Clematis

Cover photograph
Clematis 'The President'

Overleaf
Clematis texensis 'Gravetye Beauty'
Photographs by Michael Warren

Clematis

A Wisley handbook

Jim Fisk

Cassell Ltd
The Royal Horticultural Society

Cassell Ltd.
1 Vincent Square
London, SW1P 2PN
for the Royal Horticultural Society

First published 1978
New edition, fully revised and reset 1985
              second impression July 1985

British Library Cataloguing in Publication Data
Fisk, Jim
   Clematis.–New ed.
   1. Clematis
   I. Title
   635.9′33111   SB413.C6

ISBN 0-304-31078-6

Line drawings by Peter Mennim
Photographs by Jim Fisk, Michael Warren, Harry Smith
Collection, Iris Hardwick Library of Photographs
Design by Kwan Brenchley

Typeset by Georgia Origination Ltd., Formby
Printed by Canale S.p.A., Turin, Italy

Contents

Introduction and history

Clematis, these most rewarding climbers, are as tough and hardy as the British oak. They thrive anywhere in the temperate regions of the world. They belong to the Ranunculaceae, a family which includes the buttercup and anemone, and provided they are given an ample supply of water and food they are easy to grow. The only clematis native to England is *C. vitalba*, which clothes our hedges and trees in chalky areas with waves of feathery seed heads in the autumn, and is known by various nicknames such as 'old man's beard', 'traveller's joy', 'snow in harvest'. Growing as it does in chalky areas, the idea has developed that clematis can only be grown in alkaline soils, but this is a mistake as they will grow anywhere provided there is a plentiful supply of moisture and food.

The large flowered hybrids were introduced in the middle of the nineteenth century and so are a comparatively modern flower. Before this the only clematis grown were the species found growing wild in various parts of the world. The first one to be introduced to Britain came from Spain, *C. viticella*, with small purple saucer-shaped flowers, freely produced in the late summer and autumn. This plant arrived during the reign of Queen Elizabeth I of England and was given the popular name of 'the virgin's bower' in honour of the Virgin Queen. As travel became less difficult more new species began to arrive, *C. integrifolia* from Hungary in 1573, *C. cirrhosa* from the Balearic Islands in 1590, *C. recta* from south east Europe in 1597. During the next two centuries many other small flowering species were added to the list including *C. flammula*, *C. orientalis*, *C. alpina*, which are still grown today. Then in the early years of the nineteenth century plant collectors brought from China the first large flowered species, *C. patens* and *C. lanuginosa*. These were immediately used for hybridising and the first success was the very popular 'Jackmanii' raised at Jackman's Nursery at Woking in Surrey, a result of a cross between *C. lanuginosa*, *C. × eriostemon* 'Hendersonii' and *C. viticella* 'Atrorubens'. Jackmanii is still one of the most popular clematis and many a porch and trellis all over the country is covered throughout the summer with a mass of royal purple flowers. This variety has given its name to one of the

Opposite: *Clematis* × *jackmanii*

groups into which clematis have been placed, it was the first of a number of varieties with similar flowering habits, flowering for most of the summer and thus needing hard pruning during the winter, so this group is called Jackmanii. Other groups are Florida, Lanuginosa and Patens and details of their varieties will be found on pages 36–48. They have overlapped so much in the last 100 years that clematis are now listed alphabetically in most catalogues with pruning guides given to each variety.

Other large flowered hybrids quickly appeared and by the end of the nineteenth century well over 300 different varieties were on offer to the public. Less than half that number appear today in nurserymen's catalogues as many of last century's varieties were of poor colour and weak growth and have now been discarded. The best have been retained, such as 'Nelly Moser', 'The President', and 'William Kennett'. As interest in clematis has increased since the last war, new varieties of good colour and habit are constantly being added to the list, so that by the end of the twentieth century there may be almost 300 varieties once again. There are also some interesting new species collected from their native habitats in East Asia coming along which will be introduced in due course.

Clematis flower colours are mostly of a soft pastel shade, the brightest being the yellow *C. orientalis* in the species with perhaps

Clematis cirrhosa.

the vivid striped 'Dr Ruppel', and the royal purple 'Gipsy Queen' in the hybrids. They range through most of the colours, although there are no real reds or blues. The reds are all of a red wine shade, the blues all have purple or mauve in them and the nearest to yellow is a pale primrose.

Clematis can be grown in many positions in the garden, on walls, pergolas, fences and frames where they need something on which to cling such as wire or trellis. Two less usual methods of training clematis are through shrubs and trees, which after all is their natural habitat, and scrambling over wires or wirenetting laid on the ground. The sight of clematis flowers looking up at you from the ground is very effective and unusual. Both these methods are described in detail on pages 16–21.

Pruning of clematis is still a mystery with many people but the simple answer is that those varieties which flower continuously throughout the summer on the new growth are the ones that need hard pruning during the winter, and the rest can be left alone. This is dealt with in greater detail on pages 22–26.

Clematis wilt is a word to strike terror into the heart of clematis devotees, but with the appreciation of the facts that clematis are moisture loving plants, need lots of water, and that new and better fungicides are being introduced it is possible that this annoying wilting may soon be a thing of the past (see pp. 58–9).

Clematis 'Victoria'.

Above: *C. flammula*, the scented virgin's bower.
Below: *Clematis* 'Alice Fisk'.

Cultivation

Clematis like a well drained rich, crumbly loam, the perfect combination that rarely exists. However we can add manure, peat and fertilizer to our soils and when planting our clematis we can use John Innes compost No. 3 to give it a good start.

Having bought our clematis the first thing to do when the plant arrives is to make sure that the root ball is not dry. If it is, give it a good drink by soaking it in a bucket of water for an hour or two. Meanwhile prepare the planting site by digging a hole at least 18 inches (45 cm) by 18 inches wide and 18 inches deep. If the plant is to grow on a wall, then dig the hole as far away from the wall as possible – at least 9 inches (22 cm) – as the base of a wall is a very dry spot. The plant can be led to the wall by means of a cane or wire. It can even be laid in under the ground as clematis stems root freely when buried, adding to the vigour and health of the plant. (see p. 18)

When the hole is dug, break up the bottom with a fork adding two or three handfuls of bonemeal, a slow acting fertilizer which will add nutrients to the soil by the time the roots have got down that far. On top of this place a good forkful or two of manure or compost and then a spadeful of garden soil. The clematis having been well soaked is taken from its pot by turning it upside down and gently tapping the pot on the handle of a spade, holding the plant in the right hand (p.12). If it is in a paper or polythene pot, this is cut away. The roots which are long, like bootlaces, will probably have curled round the bottom of the pot and should be gently disentangled so that they can be spread out in the hole. Make sure that the ball of soil is well down in the hole so that 3 or 4 inches (7.5 to 10 cm) of the stem is *below ground* (p.18). This will produce its own roots in time and there will also be buds on this buried stem, which, in the event of an attack of wilt will shoot up and renew the life of the plant. Fill in either with John Innes compost or with your garden soil plus some peat which will help to improve moisture retention. Tread down firmly and the job is finished.

Clematis roots like to be in the shade, so if the base of your plant is in a sunny position place some slabs, tiles or stones round it, even pebbles or granite chippings will do, or if you have nothing else a mulch of peat will help to keep the roots cool and moist. To help with watering a pot sunk into the ground beside the plant,

with its rim level with the soil surface is a good idea. Water can be poured into this without running away on the surface. Liquid fertilizer can also be given this way, going straight down to the roots where it is needed.

If your plant is one of the large-flowered hybrids and has only one stem it should be cut down to the lowest pair of buds when planting. Species will break out and form a bushy plant naturally, but the large hybrids tend to go up on one stem, unless checked. Then they will break into two stems, and if these are stopped again this will make four stems. If it is one that does not need further pruning you will then have a well branched plant for the future. If it is a type to be hard-pruned then you should cut it down every winter to the lowest pair of buds on each stem, so that it naturally increases in size every year, provided it is getting enough water and fertilizer.

To keep the plant vigorous and strong an annual mulching of manure in the autumn is essential. If this is unobtainable two or three handfuls of bonemeal lightly worked in round the plant will do, with perhaps a top dressing of peat. During the spring and summer make sure that your plant has an adequate supply of water, so essential to the life of a clematis. If your soil is light and sandy, water should be given at least twice a week, not just a dribble, but a really good soak, more if it is very hot and dry. Sulphate of potash is an excellent stimulant for clematis when given in the spring. A handful round the plant, watered in well, will keep it healthy and the flowers a good colour. It will also prevent the flowers coming out green which sometimes occurs with some of the early flowering varieties such as 'Nelly Moser' and 'Mrs Cholmondeley'. Liquid manure should be given during the growing season but not when the plants are in flower, as this tends to accelerate the flowering period which is over sooner than need be. A good soaking once a week should be sufficient and any general fertilizer can be used. These can be obtained from a garden centre or shop and directions for dilution are given on each bottle.

Opposite: When the planting hole has been dug, take the plant from its pot by turning it upside down and gently knocking the pot against the spade handle.

Above: Detail of bloom of 'Vyvyan Pennell'.
Below: C. 'Vyvyan Pennell' trained over a fence.

14

Above: Clematis trained up a wall.
Below: C. *orientalis*, the "orange-peel" clematis.

Training

In the wild, the 'old man's beard' climbs by twisting its leaf stalks around the stems and twigs of bushes and trees, lifting itself to the light before producing its flowers and attractive seed heads in the summer and autumn. Their roots are hidden deep down in the shade of the hedges and this tells us that clematis like 'cool feet and hot heads'. This is the natural way to grow clematis on any bush or tree in the garden that will take them. They do no damage to their hosts, clinging to them with a firm but light grip, and grown thus they are far less likely to be damaged by gales, as they give and bend with their hosts and can ride out all but the worst storms. In this position too, they are less likely to be attacked by mildew, which in some seasons covers the Jackmanii varieties grown on walls with a grey unsightly mould. On a tree or bush they get plenty of air circulating all round them giving an environment in which the fungus does not flourish.

The beauty of growing clematis on shrubs is that, if the Jackmanii varieties are planted one can get a double show of flowers, in the spring when the shrub is blooming naturally and throughout the summer when the clematis has grown up into the shrub and produces its flowers. Many shrubs flower in May and June and so the Jackmanii varieties are ideal for this treatment as they have to be cut down every winter and so the shrub is free to produce its own flowers, before the clematis takes over. For large trees the ideal clematis is *C. montana* of which there are several forms with flowers in various shades of white and pink, and most are scented. These grow up to 30 feet (9 m) or more, and flower in May and June with thousands of star shaped dainty blooms. I have seen trees 50 and 60 feet high (15–18 m) covered in the early summer with myriads of these attractive flowers, an ideal way to cover an old or dead tree, making it a thing of beauty. These montana varieties require no pruning.

When planting on a tree or bush, plant on the shady side, so that the roots will get a certain amount of shade from the tree, and do not plant too close to the tree or bush or the clematis will have to fight for its existence. Plant as far away as is possible, at least 6 feet (1.8 m), so that the clematis roots will not have to compete with the tree roots. In orchards they will also have to compete with the grass and so it is essential that the soil around the stem of the clematis should be kept bare and free from weeds. To provide shade for the roots one could cover this bare soil with stones or granite chippings which would also help to keep the grass at bay. The clematis can be trained into the tree by means of a long bamboo cane, wires, a pole, or the stem can be laid in the ground if it is long enough to come up at the trunk of the tree. (See below.)

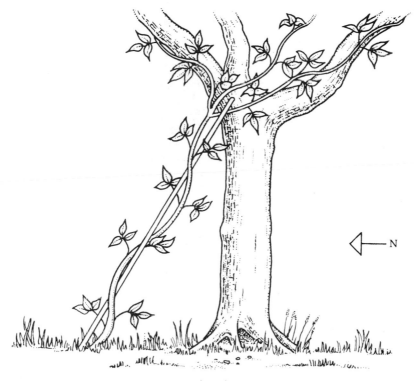

Fig. 1. Plant clematis on the north side of a tree, with the roots well clear of the tree roots. Train clematis up into the tree using a cane, pole, or wire.

Most people, however, will want a clematis to cover a wall or fence and some support must be provided for the plant to cling to and climb on as clematis do not attach themselves to the wall, but grip with their leaves. The cheapest method is to wire a wall with plastic covered wire, stretching this between nails which should be placed round the wall at 9-inch (22 cm) intervals along the top and bottom and sides. The wire is then stretched from the top nails to bottom nails all along the wall, and then from side to side so that a neat pattern of 9-inch (22 cm) squares is built up on the wall. Care must be taken, however, to keep the wire at least half an inch (1.5 cm) away from the wall, so that the leaves have space to

17

get behind the wire, twist themselves around it and get a good grip
to withstand any rough weather that may come when the plant is
in full growth. There are several excellent and handsome wire
and iron trellises available at garden centres which can be fixed to
the walls especially in prominent positions such as between
windows and doors. Wooden trellis work is also available but this
has a nasty habit of rotting and letting a plant down when in full
growth and flower.

Pergolas are another ideal situation for clematis. Permanent
ones can be built of brick piers with oak timbers as cross pieces,
expensive but extremely handsome, especially when covered
with some well grown plants which might include roses, honey-
suckle and other climbing plants as well as clematis. With a brick
pergola one must wire the piers as described for wiring a wall,
making sure that the wires are away from the brickwork, giving
the leaves space to get behind. A cheaper but very effective
pergola can be built of poles but these must be treated with wood
preservative especially the part of the pole which is put into the
ground. Creosote must not be used as the fumes from this linger
for many months and would most certainly kill a young and
tender clematis shoot. Here too wires must be used on the poles to
give the plant something to cling to.

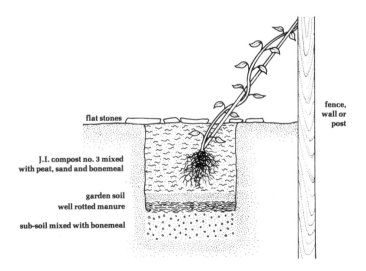

Fig. 2.   Dig a hole at least 18 ins. by 18 ins. Break up soil at base of
hole and add two or three handfuls of bonemeal. Cover this with a
layer of manure, a spadeful of garden soil, and then fill in the rest of
the hole with J.I. compost no. 3.

Above: *Clematis chrysocoma* at Windsor Great Park.
Below: *C. montana grandiflora* growing over a tripod.

Another very effective and unusual method of training clematis is to let them scramble about on the ground, to form a permanent bedding plant arrangement. Plenty of room is necessary for this method, as the best varieties to use are the Jackmanii types which flower continuously from June to October and most of them make plenty of growth during the season. However there are some varieties that do not grow more than 6 to 8 feet (1.8 to 2.4 m) such as 'Comtesse de Bouchaud', 'Hagley Hybrid' and 'Madame Edouard André', which would be ideal for such a feature in the garden. Something for them to scramble over and lift them off the ground should be provided such as wire netting, wire stretched

Clematis 'Madame Edouard André'.

between short posts or pea sticks laid on the ground. For a round bed of about 8 feet (2.4 m) across 4 or 6 plants should be used so that they can be trained over each other to hide the lower parts of the plant, which are always bare. A larger 15 feet (4.5 m) bed would need 8 or 10 plants to cover it well. Bulbs planted permanently in the bed will give colour in the spring whilst the clematis are growing. Jackmanii varieties have to be cut down during the winter, and so by the time the bulb leaves have died the clematis will have covered the bed and started to flower, to give an unusual centrepiece on the lawn. Another very effective idea is to plant the bed with winter flowering heathers. When they have established themselves the clematis can scramble over them during the summer, thus doing away with the need to provide unsightly wires or supports. With this method the bed will be a permanent feature, flowering practically throughout the year, heathers during the winter and spring and clematis all summer long. Other varieties can, of course, be used to give a spring display, such as 'Nelly Moser', 'William Kennett', and 'The President', but there is nothing during the summer. With these spring flowering varieties there is no need to prune of course, and the plants will simply grow over themselves every year eventually forming a cushion of flowers.

Other methods of training can be on tripods or poles at the back of herbaceous borders or in tubs which can be kept in the background and brought out when in flower to stand on the terrace or by the front door. Many modern houses are concreted right round the walls, making it impossible to plant anything to climb on the house. Clematis however can be grown in tubs quite successfully and these tubs can be placed at various spots and the plants trained up the walls, even on the north facing aspects as many of the early flowering varieties will do well in this position, even one or two of the summer flowering clematis such as 'Jackmanii' and 'Comtesse de Bouchaud'. Tubs must be filled with a good compost and must be kept well watered during the summer as they will dry out very quickly especially if standing in a sunny position. During the summer feed them once a week with a general liquid fertilizer as clematis are voracious feeders: in the autumn give them a handful of bone meal, and to start them off in the spring a handful of Growmore. Tubs should be at least 1½ feet deep (45 cm) and wide to give the roots plenty of room and to keep them cool some pebbles or granite chippings can be placed on top of the soil. Tubs can also be free standing in the garden with tall bamboo canes fixed to the insides of the tub and brought together to the top making a 'wigwam' for the plants to climb on, or a more ornamental iron frame can be used.

21

Pruning

Varieties that flower on the current season's wood are the only ones that need pruning, all others can be left unpruned. That, to put it briefly, is how to prune clematis. Of course if you have plenty of space you can leave them all unpruned; the only snag, however, is that the Jackmanii varieties must make a certain amount of growth before coming into flower. If unpruned they start to grow from where they flowered in the previous year, so that, unless they are being grown in trees, or with other plants on large walls, there will inevitably be bare stems at the base of the plants, and unless there is plenty of space, an untidy mass of growth high above with many flowers unable to open. This is because in a mass of untrained growth the leaves will twist round anything within their reach including many unopened buds.

The best way to deal with these varieties that flower on the young wood is to cut them down to the ground every year, down to the last pair of buds, and if they send shoots out from the ground, then completely down to the ground. This will ensure that they are green at the bottom of the plants at least, but they will make a few feet of growth before they flower. These varieties that need this hard pruning belong to the Jackmanii and Viticella groups which flower continuously throughout the summer on young wood only, and include such popular varieties as 'Comtesse de Bouchaud', 'Jackmanii Superba', 'Madame Edouard André', 'Perle d'Azur', 'Gipsy Queen', 'Ernest Markham' and 'Lady Betty Balfour'. They should all be pruned during the winter and not later than the end of February.

All the early flowering varieties flower on the previous year's wood and need no pruning, otherwise one loses those huge exotic looking flowers which appear in May and June. All one needs to do is to trim back the dead ends of the shoot in March, cutting them back with a pair of secateurs to live buds. Great care should be taken however as it is very easy to snip through a dead looking stem only to find several lovely fat buds further on. They include 'Nelly Moser', 'Lasurstern' and 'The President'. They will bloom

Opposite above: A Jackmanii clematis before pruning in winter.
Below: The same plant after pruning. The tiles in the front are to keep the roots cool.

again later in the summer on young wood with smaller and fewer flowers, but to get the spectacular display of huge plate-like flowers in the early summer do not prune. There is no hard and fast rule, however, and if you want to cut them down in the winter then all that happens is that you lose the early summer magnificence, but instead you get a good show of smaller flowers later in the summer. These early flowering varieties belong to the Patens group (which flower in May and June) and do not flower at all during the summer, but flower again in September and October on the young wood they have produced during the season.

There is another group which has a similar flowering habit and contains such varieties as 'Duchess of Edinburgh', 'Countess of Lovelace' and 'Vyvyan Pennell'. This is the Florida group which produces double flowers on the old wood and single flowers in September on the young wood – a confusing habit, and in the autumn you may think that you have the wrong variety when it comes out single. If you like doubles then this is a group that simply must not be pruned, otherwise there will be no double flowers. But if you want to do a bit of tidying up or cutting out old

C. 'Lady Betty Balfour', a very good late-flowering hybrid.

wood, then the time to do this is directly after the double blooms are over, about mid-June. You can then cut back as hard as you like and the plant will have all the rest of the summer to produce new wood ready for flowering next spring. Give the plants a good soaking beforehand of a high nitrogen liquid manure and again after the drastic pruning to encourage new growth, and feed and water well throughout the summer.

Another group which is not quite so easy to put into a pruning category is the Lanuginosa group, one of the largest, which includes such popular varieties as 'Henryi', 'Mrs Cholmondeley', 'Madame le Coultre', 'William Kennett' and 'Xerxes' (also known as 'Elsa Spath'). These flower on last season's ripened wood, in June and July, but new growth is produced while they are in flower and this continues to produce flowers during the summer at varying periods and with varying intensity, some varieties such as 'Mrs Cholmondeley' being seldom out of flower and with quite a good show at that. So how do we prune this group? If there is the space for them to grow leave them unpruned, so that you get the best of both worlds, the large early flowers and the medium sized

C. 'Lasurstern', a very popular deep blue variety.

Clematis 'Henryi', a pure white bloom.

ones in the summer. If, however, space is limited and you want flowers in the summer rather than late spring, then treat them as the Jackmanii group and prune hard during the winter. You will then get smaller flowers from June to October.

The small flowered species need little or no pruning, but here again if space is limited the early flowering ones such as *C. montana* can be cut back directly after flowering, giving them all the summer in which to produce new wood. If you have unlimited room, leave them alone and the result will be charming. Pruning is only needed when they get quite out of hand. Late flowering clematis such as *C. viticella* can be pruned during the winter. They flower on the young wood and so can be treated as the Jackmanii group, but if space is unlimited let them weave their own ways to delight us all in the autumn. Varieties such as *C. heracleifolia* and *C. texensis* are semi-herbaceous and die down naturally during the winter. All that needs to be done to these varieties is to remove the dead wood during the winter, and they will shoot from the base in the following spring.

Propagation

LAYERING

The easiest way to propagate clematis is by layering. For this, one needs a well established plant, with several stems coming from the base. Layering can be done at any time during the summer, but August is about the right time as by then any new shoots will have had time to ripen and will not snap off when bent down to the ground.

Take some flower pots, about 5 inches (12 cm) in diameter (at the top), as many as there are shoots to be layered, and some good compost to fill the pots with, John Innes No. 3 with some sharp sand mixed in would be ideal. With a sharp knife, some medium strength hormone rooting powder and pieces of wire bent in the shape of a hairpin, we are ready to start. Bend the selected shoot down to the ground, and where it touches the ground comfortably, dig a hole large enough to take a flower pot. Fill this pot with the compost and place it in the hole so that the rim is just below soil level. Bend the shoot down and where the stem can be easily pressed into the flower pot cut off an inch-long strip of the bark with a sharp knife, taking care to remove only a thin sliver of bark. Dust this cut with hormone powder, press the stem into the pot with one of the pieces of wire to hold it there safely. This means that the cut stem is below the prepared soil with the end of the shoot sticking out, which will later be the new plant. Cover the

Fig. 3.   Layering: fill a flowerpot with good compost, bend the selected shoot down and peg firmly into the pot (having first removed a small sliver of bark). Cover the pot with soil and then a large stone or brick.

pot with soil taken from the hole and firm gently. A stone or brick placed on top of the soil will prevent the layer from springing up. Leave the pots where they are for at least a year, keeping the soil moist during dry spells. To test if the layer has rooted give a tug to the shoot that is sticking out of the soil, if it feels firm then the pot will be full of roots. The stem between the parent plant and the pot can then be severed, and you have a young clematis in a pot all ready for planting in a new position, or to give as a present to a gardening friend.

CUTTINGS

This is another easy method of propagation, and clematis are unusual in that they will root from any part of the stem and do not need a heel or node at the bottom of the cutting. With most clematis the distance between nodes is rather long, and so it is as well that they will strike from internodal cuttings, i.e. cuttings made without a heel of old wood or a joint or node at the bottom of the cutting, only a short piece of stem underneath the pair of leaves, one leaf to be cut off. All that is needed is one joint or node with a pair of leaves and a piece of the stem to stick into the rooting compost. The middle part of a shoot is the best for rooting, the tip being too tender and the base becoming too hard and woody. The *montana* varieties are very easy to strike and internodal cuttings can be taken during the summer. These are put into a pot with a mixture of sharp sand and peat in equal proportions, kept in a warm shady spot in the greenhouse and watered frequently. They will root in about 4 to 6 weeks, when they can be potted in a John Innes compost No. 1 and after a few more weeks into their final and larger pot. Keep in a cool greenhouse during the winter and plant out in the spring.

Cuttings of the large flowered hybrids can be a little more difficult as shoots from a plant growing in the garden are too hard for easy rooting, but with some hormone powder they may root in time, although they will take much longer to do this than the *montana* varieties. The ideal cutting wood from large flowered hybrids is a shoot taken from a one-year-old plant grown in a greenhouse. This is the way in which most clematis are propagated commercially nowadays. The young plant in its pot is grown on in a cool greenhouse in the early spring and no heat is necessary at this stage. In April or May the shoot will be 3 to 4 feet (about 1 m) high and ready for making into cuttings. Most of it will make good cutting material with the exception of the tip which will be too soft. Cut this shoot off almost at the bottom of the plant just above a node, and cut it up into sections so that there is one

Internodal cuttings, i.e. shoots cut between the leaf joints, before rooting (left) and after rooting (right).

node to each cutting. With a sharp knife, trim the stem above the node as close to the node as possible, and below the node leave about 1 to 2 inches (3 to 5 cm) of the stem. From a shoot 3 to 4 feet (1 m) long you should get five or six cuttings. A pot or tray is now filled with a mixture of sharp sand and peat or with your own particular rooting material. Press this down firmly and insert the cuttings so that the leaves are just resting on the soil. Water the cuttings in with benomyl which will keep the cuttings clean and healthy. The pot or tray of cuttings is then placed in a propagating frame in the greenhouse, with bottom heat. Inspect the cuttings every few days to see if there is any mildew or disease on the leaves, and remove any affected ones at once. Keep the cuttings moist and shaded and in a few weeks time they will have rooted. When this happens, and a gentle tug on the leaf will prove whether there are roots anchoring them or not, they can then be given more air every day until, after a few days, the propagating frame is completely open. They should then be potted into small pots in John Innes compost No. 1, with a small stick on which to climb and kept in the greenhouse for a few weeks, giving them plenty of air every day. They can finally be potted into larger pots with John Innes compost No.3, staking each plant with a 3 or 4 foot (about 1 m) cane and plunging (burying) the pots outside in the garden, so there is no need for watering. By the following spring or early summer the pots will be full of roots and the new plant can be planted in its permanent position. As they are in pots this operation can be delayed until the following autumn, but the sooner they are taken out of their pots and planted in their permanent position the better.

Cuttings can also be raised in an outside frame with no heat, and for this young wood must be used for cutting material, although in this case the mother plants should be grown outside, so that the cuttings are firmer and able to withstand the colder conditions in a cold frame. This cold frame should be a frame within a frame so that there is a space of an inch or two between the inner and the outer one (glass and sides). The cuttings are put in the inside frame which is thus kept insulated and at a fairly constant temperature. The inside frame should be made as air-tight as possible. The soil should be a light sandy mixture so that the cuttings can root easily and it should be about 1 foot (30 cm) deep so that the roots can go straight down. Cuttings for the cold frame are taken later than those from the greenhouse plants and June is usually the best time.

Having made the internodal cuttings as described above, they can be put in the frame in rows an inch or two (3 to 5 cm) apart, making sure that the leaves do not overlap as the frame is closed for several days after inserting the cuttings. This provides a good environment for any diseases so watering in the cuttings with benomyl will keep them clean and healthy. The frame should be well shaded in sunny weather. After a fortnight inspect the cuttings to see that all is well with them and whether they need watering. Remove any dead or diseased leaves and if necessary another benomyl drenching would do no harm. Close the frames again as soon as possible, but as time goes by and the cuttings begin to root air can be given gradually. Pull one of the leaves gently to see whether the cutting is rooted. Eventually by August the frames are left open all the time. The cuttings will now be making growth and in September flowers may often appear on this year's wood. A few canes placed here and there amongst the growth will keep the young shoots off the soil. In December all this growth can be cut away, and the rooted cuttings lifted carefully with a fork. The roots will be about a foot (30 cm) long, so great care must be taken.

Trim the young shoots back almost to the original cuttings, to the lowest pair of nodes on the new growth. They can then be potted into pots 4 or 5 inches (10–12 cm) in diameter, given 3 or 4 foot (90 to 120 cm) canes and plunged into beds outside. No protection need be given as clematis are perfectly hardy. In the spring the young shoots will appear from below the ground and these are carefully tied to their canes. During the summer keep the young plants well watered and give a good liquid feed once a

Clematis orientalis (see p. 56) showing flowers and seed heads.

week. By the end of the summer the plants will be fit to plant out in their permanent sites.

GRAFTING

This is another method which the amateur may like to try. This method was used a great deal by nurserymen several years ago, but cuttings are so much easier now, that very little grafting is done. The advantage with this method is that you get a well established plant in flower within 4 months. This is because the scion is grafted on to a two-year-old rootstock, C. *vitalba*, so once the union takes place the scion has all the vigour of a two-year-old plant. Grafting has been discouraged by many people as it is thought that such plants may be more susceptible to clematis wilt. This is not so, as when a young grafted plant is potted into its final 5-inch (12 cm) pot it is planted low down in the pot so that the union is well below soil level; this encourages the scion to send out its own roots. By the end of the year the clematis is on its own roots, the rootstock eventually dying and disappearing. Grafting therefore is really a nursing of the scion until it is able to look after itself, and thus we are able to get an established plant in half the time taken by cuttings or layers.

The rootstocks used for grafting clematis are *Clematis vitalba* raised from seed sown in spring in a frame or in drills in the garden. They germinate fairly quickly and by the autumn the young seedlings can be transplanted to give them a chance to make a good root system. When the stock is two years old it is ready for grafting. The young plants can be dug up in January and taken into an unheated greenhouse and their roots covered with peat or soil to encourage them into gentle growth. At the same time, plants of the variety we wish to graft are brought into a greenhouse with heat averaging from 50 to 60°F (10–15°C). They are cut down to the lowest pair of nodes and the shoots which they produce are grown on until March when they will be about 3 feet (1 m) high. A warm propagating frame in the greenhouse is made ready for the grafts, a place where they can be kept close and warm with soil heating and an average temperature of 65°F. (18.5°C).

The rootstocks are now brought into the greenhouse, are washed for cleaner handling and are then ready for grafting. The variety to be grafted is cut down and cut into pieces each with a node. Some short thin pieces of raffia about 6 inches (15 cm) long and moistened, are ready for tying the scion to the stock. Take the root and with a sharp knife cut off all the top growth, fairly low down on to a suitable straight piece of root. Clematis are always grafted on to the root, never the stem and so no suckers appear and in any case this root dies within a year or two leaving the plant on its own roots. Pare off a thin sliver from the side of this root about an inch (2.5 cm) long. Take the pair of leaves on the node of the variety to be grafted and cut down in between the nodes. This will give you two scions, each with a leaf and a bud at the bottom of the leaf stalk. Trim off the scion to fit the cut on the root, marry them together and with the thin damp raffia bind them together starting above the leaf and continue binding until you reach the bottom of the scion where you finished off with a halfhitch. Trim off the top of the graft and plant it into a small pot 2 to 3 inches (5 to 7.5 cm) in diameter, in John Innes compost No. 1, so that the leaf and union is just above the soil. It is much easier to pot up the graft after the operation, rather than have the root already in the pot. The grafts are then placed into the warm propagating frame which is kept shut for three or four weeks. Look at them occasionally to make sure they are all right. They will not require much watering if the soil was moist when they were potted, but an occasional fine spray on hot days will help to keep the leaves turgid. In about a month's time, the bud at the bottom of the leaf stalk will start to grow, and when this is about an inch (2.5 cm) high, the pot can be taken from the propagating frame, a small thin stick given to it for support and stood on the bench in the greenhouse. When a few inches high the young plant can be stopped by pinching out the growing tip which encourages it to make a bushy plant. In a few weeks it will be a nice sturdy young plant and can be potted into a larger pot in John Innes compost No.3 and given a 3 or 4 foot (1 m) cane, but

The clematis immediately after grafting: the cut surfaces of scion and rootstock are kept closely together by a raffia tie.

this time instead of leaving the union out of the soil it is essential that it is buried below the soil. This will encourage the scion to root and eventually to grow on its own roots. By July the plant will be at the top of its cane and in most cases in flower, and it can be planted out in the garden or plunged in the soil outside ready for autumn planting.

SEED SOWING

Seed is the other method of propagating clematis but is rarely used except for producing new varieties. Only a few clematis come true from seed and these are among the species, C. *tangutica*, C. *flammula*, and C. *integrifolia* being three of them. No large flowered hybrids will come true from seed and whereas the species will germinate the same year, hybrids often take up to three years to sprout and even then 99% will be of poor flower colour and have to be rejected. It is a fascinating job to try to produce a new variety by hybridization, however, and although the chances are small there is the possibility of producing and naming a new variety and persuading a nurseryman to introduce it in his catalogue for you. If time is not important, then the procedure is this:

Select the two varieties you wish to use as parents for your new clematis, making sure that they will both flower at about the same time. The variety that is to bear the seed must not be allowed to open its sepals, otherwise it might be pollinated by a different variety, so as soon as a bud is about to open, cut off all the sepals (clematis have no petals), the stamens and anthers which produce the pollen, leaving only the stigma on the end of the pistil. This is then covered with a polythene or muslin bag to prevent any stray pollen getting on to the stigma, which in a few days time will be in a receptive state to receive the pollen from the chosen second parent. When the stigma is covered with a sticky fluid and looks shiny, then it is ready for the transfer of pollen. On a sunny day bring the flower from the chosen pollen parent, which should be full out, to the stigma and gently dust with pollen, which can be removed by shaking or with a camel hair brush. Tie a label round the stem with the names of the varieties that have been crossed. Then replace the bag over the stigma and leave for a few days to make sure that fertilization has taken place, and that there is no risk of stray pollen being transferred. Remove the bag and leave to ripen naturally.

The seed will be ripe by the autumn and can either be sown directly into trays in a seed compost or kept in a dry place and sown in the spring. The seed trays should be kept in a cool frame or greenhouse, and if nothing appears during the first year they can be placed outside for the winter, leaving them to weather, through frost and snow which may encourage them to germinate the following spring. When this happens pot each seedling into a good compost and grow on in a cool greenhouse until it is fit to plunge outside in its pot. It may flower the next year, or you may have to wait for two years before seeing a bloom, which may be a winner, or (nine times out of ten) no good at all, but it is a fascinating occupation. Even if your new flower is no good commercially you can always plant it in the garden and treasure it as your own creation.

ROOT DIVISION

There are a few herbaceous varieties which can be increased by means of root division, which is done in the winter. They are *C. heracleifolia davidiana*, *C. integrifolia* and *C. recta*, see pages 55–56. They make a bush varying in height from 2 to 4 feet (60–120 cm) and they look nothing like the popular idea of a clematis. They make an interesting addition to the herbaceous border flowering in the late summer.

Clematis heracleifolia davidiana.

The best of the hybrid clematis

The following list of the best large flowered varieties is divided up into three sections giving the fifteen best for spring flowering, fifteen for late spring and summer flowering and fifteen for summer and autumn flowering, with a brief description of the colour and approximate height. With this list one can choose one or two from each section and so have continuous flowering from May until October.

SPRING FLOWERING HYBRIDS

These are all cultivars which produce those huge magnificent blooms 6 to 8 inches (15 to 20 cm) in diameter with 8 or more sepals in the spring on the previous years ripened wood. They need no pruning, flowers appear all at once and so the general effect is dramatic; they flower for 4 to 6 weeks from about the middle of May to the middle of June. There is second flowering in September on young wood, but then the blooms are smaller and fewer. All of these will grow in any aspect.

Alice Fisk. Wisteria-blue with brown stamens. In May and June the flowers have eight broad pointed sepals but in late summer they have only six. 8 to 12 feet (2.4 to 3.6 m).

Barbara Dibley. Glowing petunia-red with deep carmine bars and dark stamens. Eight sepals which are long and pointed. Not a very free flowering variety but extremely handsome. 8 to 12 feet (2.4 to 3.6 m). (See p.38.)

Beauty of Worcester. A striking deep blue double variety with white stamens, produces single flowers on the young wood in September. 8 to 12 feet (2.4 to 3.6 m).

Bees' Jubilee. Mauve-pink with a deep carmine central bar on each sepal with brown stamens produced in great profusion. 8 to 12 feet (2.4 to 3.6 m).

Dr Ruppel. A very striking variety, rose-madder with a deep carmine bar and golden stamens. 8 to 12 feet (2.4 to 3.6 m). (See p. 39.)

Duchess of Edinburgh. Double white with many layers of sepals and yellow stamens. Before opening the bud is surrounded by curious green organs, half leaf, half flower, 8 to 12 feet (2.4 to 3.6 m).

H. F. Young. One of the best blue clematis. Masses of large wedgwood-blue flowers with cream stamens. The plant is covered in flower from top to bottom; 8 to 12 feet (2.4 to 3.6 m). (See p. 40.)

Kathleen Dunford. An unusual variety, semi-double but with both layers of sepals exactly the same size. Rich rosy purple with golden stamens, 8 to 12 feet (2.4 to 3.6 m)

C. 'Bees Jubilee', a beautiful spring-flowering hybrid.

Lasurstern.   Deeper blue than 'H. F. Young' and with larger flowers. This magnificent variety has been popular for many years; 8 to 12 feet (2.4 to 3.6 m).

Louise Rowe.   A unique variety bearing double, semi-double and single flowers all at the same time in early summer. A beautiful pale mauve with golden stamens. 6 to 8 feet (1.8 to 2.4 m). (See p.38.)

37

Above: *Clematis* 'Barbara Dibley'.
Below: *Clematis* 'Louise Rowe', a variety which bears double, semi-double and single flowers simultaneously.

Right: Detail of autumn flowers
of *Clematis* 'Dr Ruppel'.
Below: 'Dr Ruppel' growing
up a wire support.
Note the early summer
flowers with white margins.

Above: *Clematis* 'H. F. Young' is one of the best blue, spring-flowering hybrids, and is often covered with bloom from top to bottom.

Miss Bateman. Pure white with chocolate red stamens; when first opening each sepal has a green bar down the centre which fades after a few days. Not quite so large as the other varieties in this section but very free flowering, 6 to 8 feet (1.8 to 2.4 m).

Mrs N. Thompson. Vivid contrast of colour. Deep violet with a vivid scarlet bar down the centre of each sepal with deep red stamens. Very free flowering, 8 to 12 feet (2.5 to 3.6 m)

Mrs Spencer Castle. Large double flowers of a very attractive heliotrope-pink with golden stamens. Single in the autumn on young wood. 12 to 16ft (3.6 to 4.9 m).

Nelly Moser. One of the most popular clematis. Huge flat flowers of pale pink with a deep carmine stripe to each sepal, although unfortunately it fades quickly in full sun. Planted on a north facing wall or in a shady spot, the colour will last longer. Very free flowering once it has settled in after the first year or two. 8 to 12 feet (2.4 to 3.6 m). (See p. 63.)

Vyvyan Pennell. A magnificent violet-blue double with crimson shadings and golden stamens. In the autumn it produces single lavender-blue flowers, 8 to 12 feet (2.4 to 3.6 m).

LATE SPRING AND SUMMER FLOWERING HYBRIDS

These flower on the previous year's ripened wood in late spring, and throughout the summer on young wood. The early flowers have eight sepals and are 6 to 8 inches (15 to 20 cm) in diameter or even up to 10 inches (25 cm) wide. The late flowers have 6 sepals and are smaller but are produced in quite good numbers. They are best with no pruning; if space is limited they can be pruned hard in the winter, sacrificing the large early flowers. All these varieties will grow in any aspect.

General Sikorski. Striking mid-blue with crenulated edges to the sepals. Very free flowering. Golden stamens. 8 to 12 feet (2.4 to 3.6 m).

Henryi. A huge stiff pure white flower with dark stamens making a very effective bloom which will last up to three weeks in water. 12 to 20 feet (3.6 to 6 m).

John Warren. Very large flat flower, carmine-pink shading on a french-grey base with deep carmine edges. Dark stamens. 6 to 8 feet (1.8 to 2.4 m).

Lady Northcliffe. Deep lavender-blue medium-sized flowers, with white stamens, constantly in bloom all the summer. An ideal plant for the small garden as it rarely if ever exceeds 6 feet (1.8 m) in height. (See p. 42.)

Marie Boisselot. Also known as 'Madame le Coultre'. Large pure white with overlapping sepals and yellow stamens making a nice full flower. Very free flowering over a long period. 12 to 16 feet (3.6 to 4.8 m). (See p. 59.)

Mrs Cholmondeley. Lavender-blue with long pointed sepals tipped with a deeper mauve and brown stamens. One of the longest flowering of all clematis, and seldom out of flower from May to September. 12 to 16 feet (3.6 to 4.8 m).

Niobe. Deep ruby-red, almost black on first opening. Golden stamens. 6 to 8 feet. (1.8 to 2.4 m). (See p. 42.)

Ramona. Also known as hybrida Seiboldii. Rich lavender-blue with wavy sepals and dark stamens, very vigorous and free flowering. 10 to 20 feet. (3 to 6 m).

Sealand Gem. Rosy mauve with a deeper bar and brown stamens, medium size flower with attractive wavy sepals. Very free flowering. 8 to 12 feet (2.4 to 3.6 m).

Silver Moon. A very attractive colour. Mother of pearl grey with yellow stamens. Very free flowering. 8 to 12 feet (2.4 to 3.6 m). (See p. 44.)

The President. Deep purple-blue with reddish purple stamens. A very handsome flower rarely out of bloom during the season. 8 to 12 feet (2.4 to 3.6 m).

Violet Charm. Rich violet with long pointed sepals. A well shaped flower constantly in bloom and an ideal plant for small gardens. 6 to 8 feet (1.8 to 2.4 m).

W. E. Gladstone. The largest flower of all, often 10 inches (25 cm) across. Lilac-blue with purple stamens. A magnificent variety. 8 to 12 feet (2.4 to 3.6 m).

William Kennett. Deep lavender-blue with dark purple stamens. The sepals are overlapping and crenulated making a very handsome bloom. Very free flowering over a long period. 10 to 20 feet (3 to 6 m).

Xerxes. Also known as 'Elsa Spath'. Deep violet-blue with purple shadings to the rounded sepals; dark stamens. Very free flowering variety, seldom out of bloom. 8 to 12 feet (2.4 to 3.6 m). (See p. 43.)

Above: *Clematis* 'Lady Northcliffe'.
Below: *Clematis* 'Niobe'.

Above: *Clematis* 'Xerxes'
(also known as 'Elsa Spath')
on a wall.
Right: Detail of 'Xerxes'.

43

Opposite: *Clematis* 'Comtesse de Bouchaud' (see below).
Above: *Clematis* 'W. E. Gladstone'.

SUMMER AND AUTUMN FLOWERING HYBRIDS

These cultivars all bloom on the current year's growth and so need hard pruning every winter, but not later than the end of February. They flower continuously for up to three months, new buds appearing throughout the season to give an effect of non-stop flowering. The blooms are medium-sized, 4 to 6 inches (10 to 15 cm) across with 4 to 6 sepals. What they lack in size they make up for in numbers. Most varieties need a sunny aspect and will do on an east, south or west wall. 'Jackmanii', 'Comtesse de Bouchaud', 'Hagley Hybrid' and 'Victoria' will also do fairly well on north facing walls but really prefer a sunny aspect.

Comtesse de Bouchaud. Satiny-rose with cream stamens, very vigorous and reliable, flowering in great profusion all summer long. 8 to 12 feet (2.4 to 3.6 m).

Ernest Markham. Glowing petunia-red, blunt tipped sepals and golden stamens, a good late flowering variety. One of the few Jackmanii varieties that will flower in the spring on the old wood if left unpruned, but does much better if pruned hard every winter. 12 to 16 feet (3.6 to 4.8 m). (See p. 47.)

Etoile Violette. Deep purple with yellow stamens, small flowers but masses of them. 8 to 12 feet (2.5 to 3.6 m). (See p. 46.)

Gipsy Queen. Rich violet-purple with a velvet sheen, very free and vigorous. Rich violet-purple stamens. 12 to 16 feet (3.6 to 4.8 m).

Opposite: *Clematis* 'Etoile Violette'.
Top: *Clematis* 'Ernest Markham'.
Above: Detail of 'Ernest Markham'.

47

Hagley Hybrid. Beautifully shaped shell-pink flowers with brown stamens. An ideal variety for a small garden growing to about 6 feet (1.8 m). To keep its delicate colour, plant in a shady aspect.

Huldine. Pearly white translucent small flowers with a mauve bar on the reverse and pale yellow stamens. A good strong late variety and very free flowering. 12 to 20 feet (3.6 to 6 m).

Jackmanii. Masses of purple flowers with green stamens all summer. The best known clematis and popular for over 100 years. 12 to 30 feet (3.6 to 9 m).

John Paul II. Creamy-white with pink shadings which become more distinctive in late summer. Creased and overlapping firm sepals with reddish stamens.

Lady Betty Balfour. A very good late variety for a hot sunny wall, flowering in September and October. Violet-blue with yellow stamens. Vigorous and free flowering. 10 to 16 feet (3 to 4.8 m).

Madame Edouard André. Wine-red flowers, pointed sepals and cream coloured stamens. An ideal variety for the small garden growing to about 6 feet (1.8 m).

Margaret Hunt. Dusky pink with brown stamens, very vigorous and free flowering. 12 to 16 feet (3.6 to 4.8 m).

Perle d'Azur. The only pale blue variety in the Jackmanii group, semi-nodding flowers with blunt tipped corrugated sepals and green stamens. Very free flowering over a long period. 10 to 16 feet (3 to 4.8 m).

Rouge Cardinal. Glowing crimson with brown stamens, a very attractive variety, 8 to 12 feet (2.4 to 3.6 m).

Victoria. Soft heliotrope-mauve with buff stamens. A shapely flower, vigorous and free flowering. 10 to 16 feet (3 to 4.8 m).

Ville de Lyon. Carmine-red with a deep crimson shading round the edges of the sepals. Golden stamens. 12 to 16 feet (3.6 to 4.8 m). (See p. 61.)

Below: *Clematis* 'Perle d'Azur'.
Opposite: *Clematis* 'Rouge Cardinal'.

The best of the species clematis

Species are very diverse in their forms of flower, leaf and growing habits, they come from all over the temperate zones of the earth, and are plants of great value and beauty. Several of them are scented, a virtue the handsome hybrids lack. They also produce attractive seed heads from July onwards. They are trouble free, and will do well on any soil, especially on chalky soils. Very little pruning is necessary although the autumn flowering ones can be pruned back during the winter if necessary.

SPRING FLOWERING SPECIES

C. alpina. "The alpine virgin's bower" from southern Europe is a good clematis for the small garden, growing to about 6 feet (1.8 m). The beautiful satiny-blue nodding flowers with white stamens are produced in great profusion in April and May.

C. alpina 'Ruby'. Rosy-red nodding flowers with white petaloid stamens which are produced in April—May. 6 to 8ft (1.8 to 2.4 m).

Clematis alpina.

C. armandii.   A handsome evergreen clematis with large leathery three-lobed leaves. The flowers are waxy white, sweetly scented and produced in profusion in March and April. It is hardy on the coast but inland needs the shelter of a south wall. 20 to 30 feet (6 to 9 m). (See p. 52 for 'Snowdrift'.)

C. chrysocoma.   Soft pink flowers with golden stamens, similar to *C. montana* but will often flower in the summer on young shoots. Called the "Hairy Clematis" because of the fine golden hairs on the young growth. 20 to 30 feet (6 to 9 m).

C. cirrhosa balearica.   One of the few evergreen clematis, often called the fern-leaved clematis as its leaves are finely cut and feathery. It comes from the Balearic Islands and the flowers are produced during mild spells early in the year from January to March. They are small, bell-shaped and creamy white in colour. Grows to a height of from 20 to 30 feet (6 to 9 m).

C. macropetala.   The "downy clematis" is so called because its young growth is covered with fine downy hairs. It comes from China and its beautiful semi-double blue nodding flowers appear in April and May. 8 to 12 feet (2.4 to 3.6 m).

C. macropetala 'Maidwell Hall'.   A deeper blue variety. 8 to 12 feet (2.4 to 3.6 m).

C. macropetala 'Markham's Pink'.   Lavender-pink, semi-double nodding flowers with white stamens, 8 to 12 feet (2.4 to 3.6 m).

C. montana 'Elizabeth'.   The *montana* varieties are ideal for covering a wall area quickly, for growing on north facing walls or in the shade. They produce thousands of flowers in May and June. 'Elizabeth' is pale pink with yellow stamens and very sweetly scented. 20 to 30 feet (6 to 9 m).

C. montana grandiflora.   White flowers, vigorous and free flowering. 20 to 30 feet (6 to 9 m).

Clematis macropetala.

Clematis armandii 'Snowdrift'.

Clematis chrysocoma.

C. montana 'Marjorie'.   A semi double montana with creamy-pink sepals and a centre of salmon-pink petaloid stamens. 20 to 30 feet (6 to 9 m).

C. montana 'Pink Perfection'.   Perhaps the best pink form, with clear pink flowers and pale yellow stamens. 20 to 30 feet (6 to 9 m).

C. montana 'Tetrarose'.   The largest flower of the montana group, lilac rose with golden stamens. 20 to 30 feet (6 to 9 m).

C. montana 'Wilsonii'.   The last of the *montanas* to bloom, strongly scented. The creamy white flowers are produced by the thousand in June and July. The sepals are attractively twisted and the stamens are yellow and prominent. 20 to 30 feet (6 to 9 m).

C. spooneri.   Pure white flowers with yellow stamens, allied to the *montana* group. 20 to 30 feet (6 to 9 m).

Clematis spooneri.

SUMMER AND AUTUMN FLOWERING SPECIES

C. flammula. The "scented virgin's bower" which fills the garden with a delightful almond scent in the late summer and autumn. The flowers are very small, white, and produced in great profusion and are quickly followed by masses of silver-grey seed heads. 20 to 30 feet (6 to 9 m).

C. heracleifolia davidiana 'Wyevale'. One of the herbaceous clematis forming a bush 2 to 3 feet (60 to 90 cm) in height. The scented blue flowers are produced in clusters in the axil of each large leaf in the late summer. They are shaped like a hyacinth. It needs pruning during the winter.

C. integrifolia. Another herbaceous clematis, blooming during the summer with nodding flowers of a deep blue and white stamens. An ideal plant for the rockery. Needs hard pruning in the winter. 1 to 2 feet (30 to 60 cm).

C. integrifolia 'Durandii'. A taller growing variety with larger deep indigo-blue flowers. Ideal for growing through shrubs or wall climbers as it needs supporting. A semi-herbaceous variety which does not climb by twisting its leaves round its support as other clematis do. 6 to 8 feet (1.8 to 2.4 m).

Clematis integrifolia 'Hendersonii' has larger flowers than the species.

55

C. jouiniana. A semi herbaceous clematis which needs tying to its support but if left on the ground makes an excellent ground cover. Masses of small pale blue flowers in the autumn. 10 to 20 feet (6 to 9 m).

C. orientalis (LSE 13372). Orange coloured, nodding, bell-shaped flowers with very thick fleshy sepals. This one is called the "orange peel" clematis and comes from Tibet. The foliage is finely cut and an attractive grey green in colour. 10 to 20 feet (3 to 6 m).

C. recta. An herbaceous clematis forming a large bush with masses of small white sweetly scented flowers at the end of strong 3 to 4 foot (90 to 120 cm) stems; ideal for floral decoration. Prune hard every winter.

C. rehderiana. The "nodding virgin's bower", also known as *C. nutans*. This curious clematis comes from western China and is a rampant grower with coarse foliage. The small primrose coloured tubular shaped flowers hang downward in clusters, each with recurving sepals looking like trouser turn-ups. The scent however is its greatest asset, a heavenly cowslip perfume, in autumn. 10 to 20 feet (3 to 6 m). Can be pruned hard every winter. Not commonly available commercially.

Clematis recta.

Clematis rehderiana.

C. tangutica 'Gravetye'. Masses of small yellow lantern shaped nodding flowers followed by clouds of feathery seed heads in the autumn. 10 to 20 feet (6 to 9 m).

C. texensis 'Duchess of Albany'. The *texensis* varieties come from the U.S.A. and are semi-herbaceous in habit, dying down to the ground every winter. This variety produces masses of long tubular flowers throughout the summer, the colour being a good clear pink with cream stamens. 8 to 12 feet (2.4 to 3.6 m).

C. texensis 'Etoile Rose'. Beautiful bell-shaped flowers of cerise-pink with silver edges to the sepals. 6 to 8 feet. (1.8 to 2.5).

C. texensis 'Gravetye Beauty'. The deepest colour of this group, a glowing crimson, the tubular flowers gradually open out to a star-shaped flower. 8 to 12 feet (2.4 to 3.6 m).

C. viticella. The "virgin's bower". The wild clematis from Spain which gave rise to the popular name the virgin's bower being introduced during the reign of Elizabeth I. Small purple saucer-shaped flowers with brown stamens that hang downwards in great profusion. A vigorous grower. It can be pruned hard every winter if necessary. 20 to 30 feet (6 to 9 m).

C. viticella 'Minuet'. A charming variety with cream-coloured sepals edged with mauve and held upright on long stems. 10 to 20 feet (6 to 8 m).

C. viticella rubra. The best colour in the *viticella* group, a rich glowing crimson with reddish brown stamens. It is vigorous and free flowering and can be pruned hard every winter. 10 to 20 feet (3 to 6 m).

57

Diseases and pests

Diseases in clematis are few, but there is one that has caused much frustration and disappointment amongst clematis lovers and that is clematis wilt, the hybrid types being particularly prone to this trouble. Wilt is the most infuriating of all diseases, as a plant apparently in full health and vigour, often full of bud or flower will suddenly collapse overnight and be dead by the following evening. It is as though the whole plant had been cut through with a knife at the bottom and all the growth and buds hang limply down, a sorry sight, especially if in a prominent position on the house. In the past this trouble has been attributed to many different causes, such as bad drainage, malnutrition, graft failure, insect or chemical damage. In recent years, however, it has been found that the fungus *Ascochyta clematidina* can cause wilt, and is regarded by many people as the major cause of dieback in outdoor plants. The fungus enters the plant fairly low down and on closer examination of the affected parts a discoloration of the stem can be seen, or even small rotting patches, under the lowest pair of wilting leaves. Often however, these symptoms are not noticed because they occur so low down and may even be below soil level. The disease is most troublesome in wet seasons.

Wilted shoots never recover, but young healthy shoots sometimes develop below soil level, especially if the clematis was planted with two or three inches (5 or 7.5 cm) of stem below the soil, or from nodes directly beneath the wilted region. In any case the clematis plant is rarely killed outright in one season. There is no need, therefore, to dig up an affected plant, but the wilted shoots should be cut back to clean, living tissues even if this means going below soil level. The wounds, however small, should be painted with a good protective paint. Spray new shoots when produced with a copper-containing fungicide such as bordeaux mixture or liquid copper or benomyl. It is a good idea to spray all clematis plants with such a fungicide, in the autumn and again in the spring when the shoots start to develop, covering in particular the base of the plant, as this should help to prevent attacks of the disease. Do not use benomyl too often as this may damage the foliage, but these two applications will be quite safe.

Shortage of water can, of course, also lead to wilting of clematis, particularly as these plants do seem to require a lot of water.

Clematis 'Marie Boisselot'.

Clematis grown near rivers seldom, if ever, appear to wilt as they have a constant water supply underneath their roots. In a clematis stem the water vessels are large and few in number and on drier soils, in conditions of great demand for water, the root pressure is unable to force enough water to the tops of the stems and a breakdown occurs, usually at the base of the plant, cutting off all the moisture. These wood vessels are replaced every year and this breakdown could occur at the time when new ones are being developed, and if water demand is high, these would be unable to cope with the sudden demand. For people living on drier soils it has been suggested that a container buried underneath the plant, filled with stones and then topped up with water, could provide that constant supply the riverside clematis always have. The container should be large enough to hold a gallon or two of water, and when buried is covered with peat. The clematis is then planted on top of this and a pipe leading down to the container could be the means of topping up with water during dry spells. It is rather a laborious way to plant a clematis, but if effective, it is well worth the effort.

Another disease of clematis which is fortunately very rare is caused by virus. Affected plants have mottled and distorted leaves and the flowers are also malformed or of poor quality. Although these symptoms may become less obvious during the summer, the affected plant is not cured and it should be dug up and burned.

Where the soil is allowed to dry out, clematis plants are likely to be affected by another disease, namely powdery mildew, which can be troublesome in the southern counties. It shows as a white powdery deposit on the leaves and occasionally on the flowers. Powdery mildew can be checked by spraying with dinocap and other fungicides could be tried such as those having systemic properties, e.g. benomyl and thiophanate-methyl.

Another thing that sometimes worries people is the browning of the lower leaves of one or two varieties, especially the red and pink Jackmanii varieties such as 'Ville de Lyon' and 'Comtesse de Bouchaud'. This usually happens in the summer and spoils the look of the plants just when they are at their best. This is not a disease and is only the natural dying off of the early leaves. Clematis start to grow very early in the year; by mid-summer these

Clematis texensis 'Duchess of Albany'.

Clematis 'Ville de Lyon'.

early leaves have done their job and the top of the plant is well furnished with young new leaves, which are nearer to the light than those at the bottom of the plant, so the bottom ones simply die. They can be cut off, of course, but this leaves a bare stem which looks almost as bad. So if this is a problem why not grow a few tall-growing annuals in front, or the clematis can be planted behind a shrub or a rose which will help hide the brown leaves. Most clematis, however, keep their lower leaves green until the autumn.

The first flowers of the season, particularly of the cultivar 'Nelly Moser', frequently show a greenish discoloration of some or all of the petals; this is quite different from the virus described earlier in this chapter which is a mottle green and yellow leaf (often distorted), whereas with this greening the flowers are perfectly formed but simply green instead of their usual colour. The exact cause is not known, although it is believed to be due to cold weather conditions at a critical stage in the development of the flower. It can also be caused by lack of potash in the soil and a top dressing of sulphate of potash early in the year will help. On most plants which show greening of the early blooms, the later flowers develop normally.

61

In recent years another trouble which has appeared on clematis, particularly on *C. montana*, is the development of slime fluxes which show as decaying patches on the stems covered with thick, slimy yellow, pink or orange growths. The original cause of most slime fluxes on clematis is a wound, usually due to frost damage but sometimes occurring as a result of wilt disease (see above) through which some of the plant sap escapes. This being rich in sugars is colonised by yeasts, bacteria and fungi which normally do no harm. Occasionally however, the fermentation which they cause, injures the surrounding bark tissues thus extending the area of the wound and making the trouble progressively worse. Unfortunately there is no really effective method of treating a slime flux on a clematis plant apart from cutting out the affected shoots to well below the apparently diseased tissues even if this means going down below soil level. The affected plant is likely to shoot again and it should then be sprayed with a copper fungicide as recommended above for the control of clematis wilt.

Below: *Clematis montana*.
Opposite: *Clematis* 'Nelly Moser'.

With regard to pests, slugs are fond of young shoots, but they can be controlled with slug bait. Green and black fly sometimes attack clematis and the usual systemic sprays will deal with them. Holes in leaves and flowers and the ends of shoots being bitten off are often rather baffling as nothing can be seen which could cause this damage. Caterpillars can be the cause, but they can usually be seen and dealt with. The main culprits are earwigs which hide during the day in crevices and under the bark of trees, but at night come out to feed on the plant and by the morning often reduce what the day before was a beautiful flower, almost to a skeleton. If a torch is taken after dark one can see these pests covering the plant, enjoying their midnight feast. The best time to spray these insects then is after dark. If this cannot be done, spray the whole plant, leaves, flowers and stems, with BHC as late in the evening as possible, so that the whole plant is thoroughly wet and will stay wet whilst the pests come out. A few sprays like this will at least deter them, if not actually doing away with them altogether.

Further reading

Lloyd, Christopher. Clematis. Collins, London, 1977.

Specialist Nurseries

Fisk's Clematis Nursery, Westleton, Nr Saxmundham,
    Suffolk, 1P17 3AJ
Christopher Lloyd, Great Dixter, Northiam,
    Nr Rye, E. Sussex
Pennell & Sons Ltd., Beant Road, Lincoln LN5 9AF
Peveril Clematis Nursery, Derril,
    Nr Holsworthy, Devon
Treasures' of Tenbury Ltd., Tenbury Wells,
    Worcestershire WR15 8HQ